Share It!

1

Student Book

Nicholas Beare

macmillan education

Scope & Sequence

Welcome to Shareville! pages 4–5	Hi, Hello Character names: Alex, Eva, Nancy, May, Dan, Sam, Sally	I'm … My name's … What's your name?	*Share It!* Song
	Vocabulary	**Grammar**	**Sharebook**
Unit 1 **At School** pages 10–19	clock, window, board, desk, picture, chair, notebook, backpack book, pencil, crayon, pen, pencil sharpener, pencil case, ruler, eraser	What's this? It's a / an … Is it a / an …? Yes, it is. / No, it isn't.	*What's This?* Sharebook pages 7, 9 *Guess and Draw* Sharebook pages 11, 12
Unit 2 **Family and Friends** pages 20–29	grandma, grandpa, brother, sister, dad, mom, friend truck, bike, ball, robot, car, doll, kite	Who's this? This is my … How many …? What color are they? They're …	*Family Pictures* Sharebook page 13 *How Many Toys?* Sharebook pages 15, 16
Share the World 1	**Poem:** *A Surprise for You!* pages 30–31		
Unit 3 **Jobs** pages 34–43	farmer, teacher, vet, artist, doctor, cook firefighter, pilot, bus driver, dentist, astronaut, singer, police officer, mail carrier	He's / She's a … He / She isn't a … Is he / she a …? Yes, he / she is. No, he / she isn't.	*Find Four Differences* Sharebook pages 17, 18 *Guess the Job* Sharebook pages 19, 21
Unit 4 **At Home** pages 44–53	bathroom, bedroom, living room, dining room, kitchen, yard, garage TV, closet, bed, sofa, bathtub, lamp, refrigerator, rug	Where's your …? He's / She's in the … Where are your …? They're in / on / under / next to the …	*Find Your Friends!* Sharebook pages 23, 24 *Find the Differences* Sharebook pages 25, 26
Share the World 2	**Story:** *The Red Envelope* pages 54–55		
Unit 5 **My Pets** pages 58–67	turtle, fish, snake, cat, bird, spider, mouse, dog old, young, long, short, big, small, ugly, cute	I have a … I don't have a … Do you have a …? Yes, I do. / No, I don't. I have three …	*Who Am I?* Sharebook page 27 *Go Fish!* Sharebook pages 29, 31
Unit 6 **At the Fair** pages 68–77	head, hand, arm, leg, feet, fingers eyes, ears, nose, mouth, hair, teeth	He / She / It has … He / She / It doesn't have … Does he / she / it have …? Yes, he / she / it does. No, he / she / it doesn't.	*Guess the Robot* Sharebook page 33 *Three Questions* Sharebook page 35
Share the World 3	**Article:** *Koalas Are Cute!* pages 78–79		
Unit 7 **At the Park** pages 82–91	women, men, lake, picnic table, children, swings, slide, seesaw numbers 11–20	There's … There are … How many … are there?	*Find Five Differences* Sharebook pages 37, 38 *Animal Lake* Sharebook pages 39, 40
Unit 8 **A Picnic** pages 92–101	meat, ice cream, cheese, candy, bread, salad, cake, pizza milk, yogurt, water, juice, rice, fish, fruit	I like … I don't like … Do you like …? Yes, I do. / No, I don't.	*I Like It!* Sharebook pages 41, 43 *The Food Quiz* Sharebook page 45
Share the World 4	**Play:** *Picnic in the Jungle* pages 102–103		
Grammar Practice	pages 106–109		

Welcome Unit pages 6–9

Our Classroom
orange, pink, purple, green, brown, black, yellow, blue, red, white
numbers 1–10, the alphabet

What color is it?
How old are you?
How do you spell …?

Reading	CLIL	Phonics	Progress Tracker
Story *Let's Share!* **Value** Share!	**Art** **Text:** *Shapes* circle, square, rectangle, triangle, heart **Project:** Picture of shapes in the classroom	*Aa, Bb, Cc*	Review Game: *Spin to Win!*
Story *Happy Birthday, Alex!* **Value** Be polite!	**Social Studies** **Text:** *Families* man, woman, boy, girl, people **Project:** Picture of family	*Dd, Ee, Ff*	Review Game: *Race to Win!*
Exam Practice 1 Listening, Reading and Writing pages 32–33			
Story *I'm Sorry, Eva!* **Value** Say sorry!	**Social Studies** **Text:** *Jobs in the Community* taxi, motorcycle, fire truck, plane **Project:** Poster of jobs in the community	*Gg, Hh, Ii*	Review Game: *Four in a Row!*
Story *Hide and Seek!* **Value** Show respect!	**Social Studies** **Text:** *Houses in Nature* flowers, tree, water, plants **Project:** Picture of a house in nature	*Jj, Kk, Ll*	Review Game: *Round and Round!*
Exam Practice 2 Listening, Reading and Writing pages 56–57			
Story *Animals Are Friends* **Value** Be nice!	**Art** **Text:** *Drawing with Shapes* peacock, panda, squirrel, iguana **Project:** Animal picture drawn with shapes	*Mm, Nn, Oo*	Review Game: *Spin to Win!*
Story *Look Out, Dan!* **Value** Be careful!	**Science** **Text:** *The Five Senses* see, smell, hear, touch, taste **Project:** Pictures of favorite things to see, smell, hear, touch, and taste	*Pp, Qq, Rr*	Review Game: *Race to Win!*
Exam Practice 3 Listening, Reading and Writing pages 80–81			
Story *Wash Your Hands!* **Value** Help others!	**Math** **Text:** *Math in English!* equation, plus, equals, minus **Project:** Math quiz	*Ss, Tt, Uu, Vv*	Review Game: *Four in a Row!*
Story *Are You OK?* **Value** Eat healthy!	**Health** **Text:** *Eat a Rainbow!* healthy, meal, rainbow **Project:** Food rainbow poster	*Ww, Xx, Yy, Zz*	Review Game: *Round and Round!*
Exam Practice 4 Listening, Reading and Writing pages 104–105			
Word List pages 110–111			

Welcome to Shareville!

1 1.01 **Read and listen.**

2 1.02 **Listen and sing.**

Share It! Song

Everybody, clap along
Clap your hands to the *Share It* Song!
Let's be fair, and show we care
All together now, let's share!

Come to Shareville, we'll learn today
And make some friends along the way
We'll share the world, we all belong
Share our voices and all sing this song!

Welcome Unit

Our Classroom

1 Listen and read. Then talk about it.

1 Be respectful!

Listen to the teacher.

Raise your hand.

2 Be kind!

Share your things.

Take turns.

3 Be responsible!

Finish your work.

Clean up.

2 Read and think. Then write your name.

I promise to be respectful, kind, and responsible.
I promise to follow our classroom rules.

Name: ______________________________

Workbook page 4

3 1.04 **Listen, point, and say.**

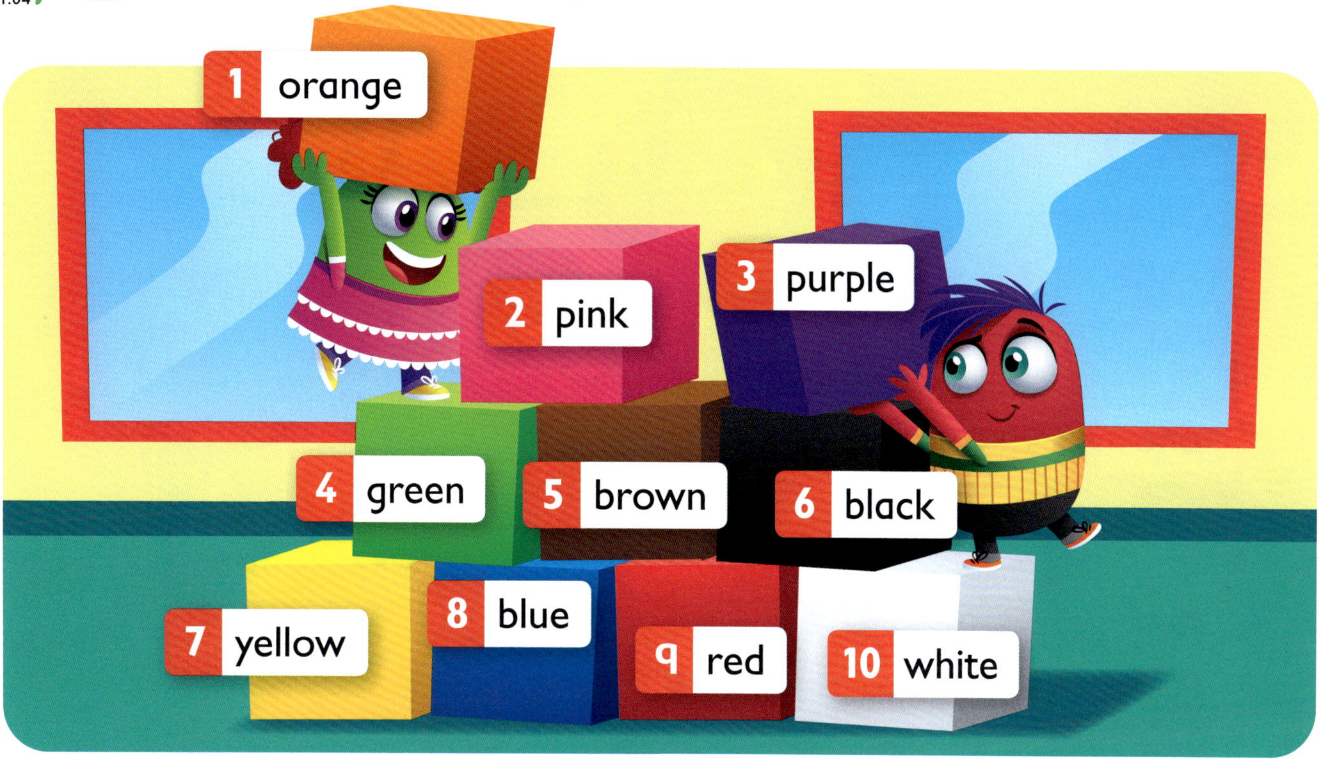

4 1.05 **Listen, point, and chant.**

Yellow, green, black, red,
Brown and blue,
Orange and purple,
Pink and white, too.

5 1.06 **Listen, read, and say.**

Workbook page 5

I can name colors.

Numbers

6 1.07 **Listen, point, and say. Then quiz a friend.**

7 1.08 **Listen, read, and say.**

8 1.09 **Listen, point, and say. Then sing the Alphabet Song.**

9 1.10 **Listen, read, and say.**

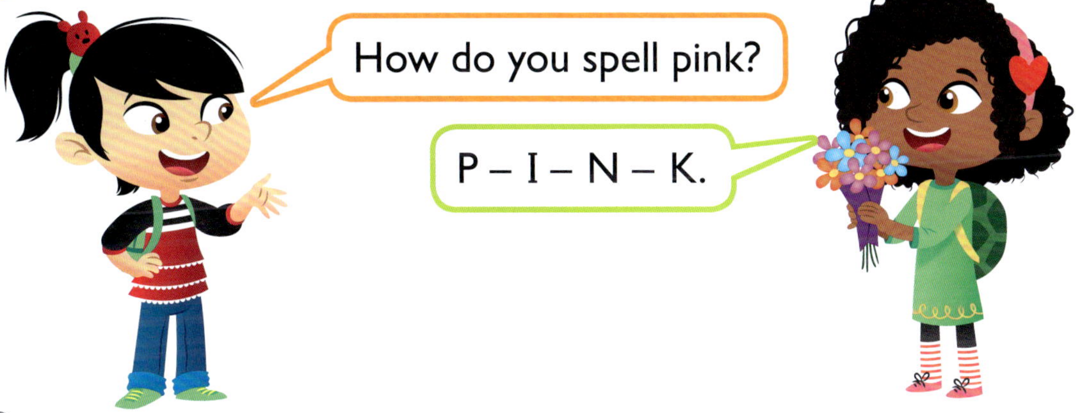

10 1.11 **Listen and read the poem.**

I Can!

I can draw.
I can paint, too.
I can spell,
And say the alphabet, too!

I can sing.
I can dance, too.
I can clap,
And say the alphabet, too!

Workbook page 7

I can say the alphabet. ☐

1 At School

Lesson 1 Vocabulary

1 Talk about the picture.

What color is this?

It's yellow.

2 (1.12) **Listen, point, and say. Then quiz a friend.**

3 (1.13) **Listen and point. Then chant.**

Look at the clock.
It's time for school!
A chair, a desk,
A big board, too!

A window, a picture,
Look! How cool!
A backpack, a notebook,
I like school!

 I can name things at school. ☐

Workbook page 8

Lesson 2 Grammar

1 (1.14) **Listen to May and Dan. Then read and say.**

Grammar

What's this?

It's a backpack.

a backpack / **an o**range backpack

What**'s** = What **is** It**'s** = It **is**

Grammar Practice page 106

2 (1.15) **Listen and point. Then ask and answer.**

3 Sharebook A: page 7 B: page 9

What's This?

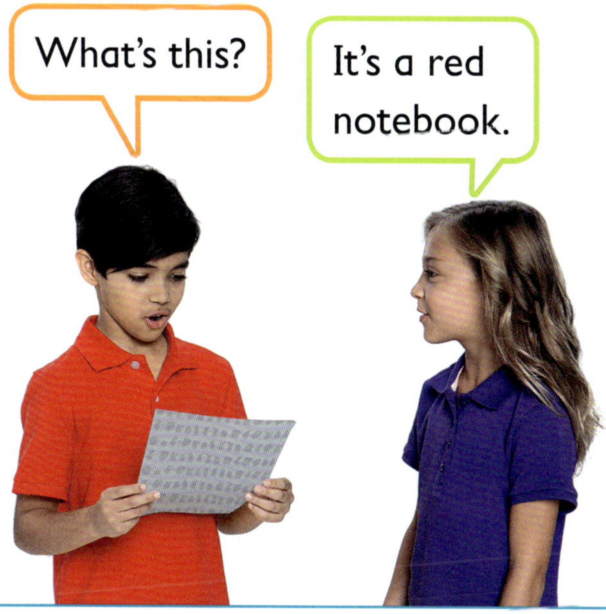

I can ask and answer about things at school. ☐

Lesson 3 Story Let's Share!

1 Look and circle.

Nancy shares her desk. Yes / No

2 1.16 **Read the story. Then act.**

Value
Share!

3 Look, read, and check (✓). Who shares?

1 Nancy ☐

2 Dan ☐

3 May ☐

Workbook page 10

I can read the story. ☐

Lesson 4 Vocabulary

1 1.17 **Listen, point, and say. Then quiz a friend.**

1 book

2 pencil

3 crayon

4 pen

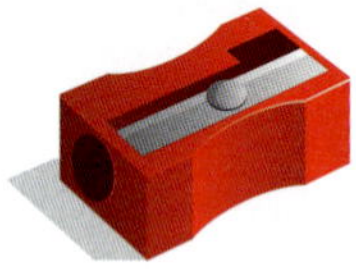

5 pencil sharpener

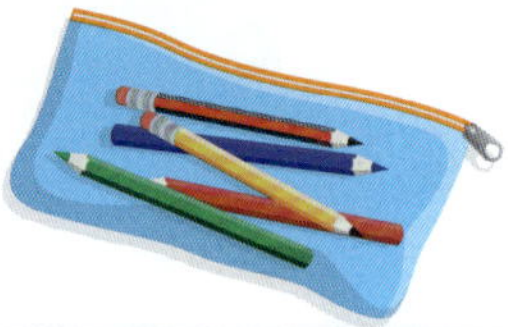

6 pencil case

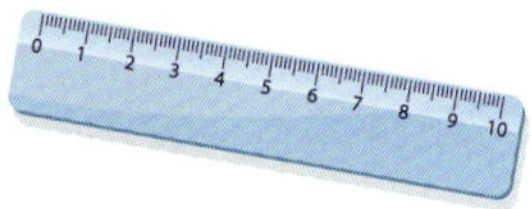

7 ruler

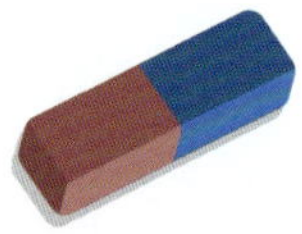

8 eraser

2 1.18 **Listen and point. Then sing.**

Put It In Your Pencil Case!

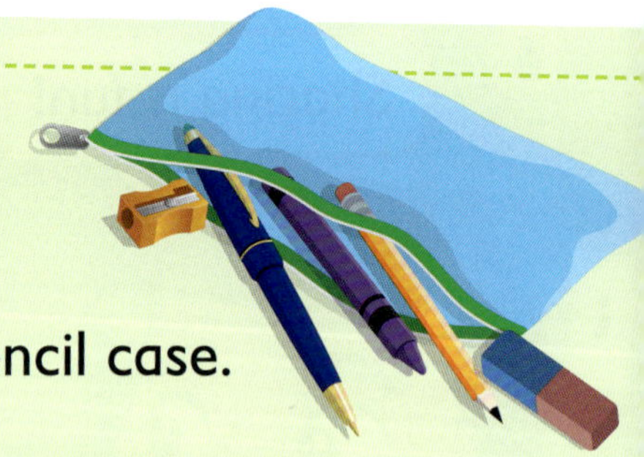

A crayon, a pencil, a ruler, a pen.
Show me! It's fun!
An eraser, a pencil sharpener,
a book.
Good! Well done!

Pick up your pencil case.
Let's play!
Put your crayon in your pencil case.
Yes! OK!
Put your book in your pencil case.
No! No way!

3 **Point, ask, and answer.**

What's this?

It's a green pencil.

 I can name school supplies. ☐ Workbook page 11

1 Listen, read, and say.

1.19

2 Listen and number.

1.20

a

☐

b
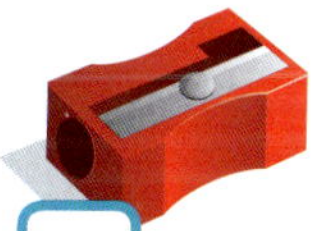
☐

c

☐

Grammar

Is it a pencil sharpener?

Yes, it **is**. **No**, it **isn't**.

is**n't** = is **not**

Grammar Practice page 106

3 Sharebook *Guess and Draw*

A: page 11
B: page 12

Workbook page 12 I can ask and answer about school supplies. ☐

Lesson 6 Art CLIL

1 Look. How many shapes can you see?

2 (1.21) Read the text. What shape is the ruler?

Shapes

1 This window is a **circle**.

2 The board is a **square** and the book is a **rectangle**.

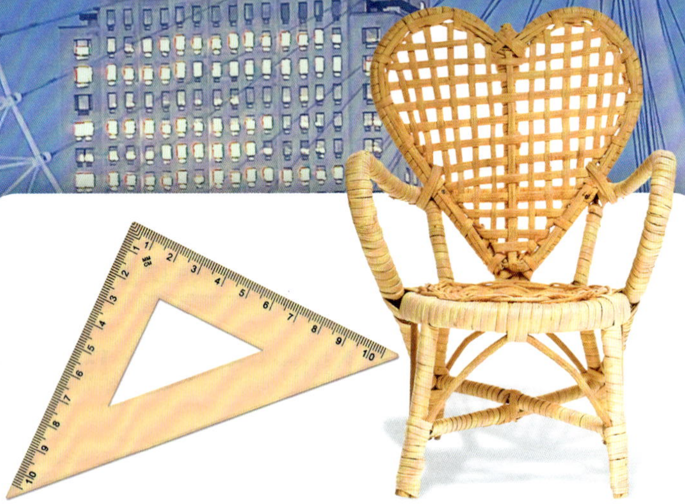

3 Look! The ruler is a **triangle**. The chair is a **heart**.

Can you see shapes around you?

 I can read about shapes. ☐

Workbook page 13

1 (1.22) **Read the text again.**

2 Read and match.

1 circle
2 square
3 rectangle
4 triangle
5 heart

a 
b 
c 
d 
e 

3 Project Look for shapes in your classroom. Draw a picture.

4 Share it! Talk about your picture with the class.

It's a window. It's a rectangle.

Share at Home
Find five shapes at home and say the names.

I can share my picture. ☐

Lesson 8 Phonics Aa, Bb, Cc

1 Listen, point, and chant.

1.23

2 Listen and repeat. Then read and say.

1.24

1	A	a	B	b	C	c
2	b	C	a	c	A	B

REVIEW

3	B	C	A	F	D	E
4	a	b	f	e	c	d

3 Look and listen. Circle the first letter.

1.25

1 a b c

2 a b c

3 a b c

4 a b c

5 a b c

4 Listen, read, and say.

1.26

The car is black,
The ball is blue,
The book is brown,
And the ant is, too!

 I can read the letters Aa, Bb, and Cc. ☐

Workbook page 15

1 Play *Spin to Win!* Use the language from Unit 1.

How to Play

1 Spin with a pencil and paper clip.

2 Look, read, and answer.

3 Don't know? Lose a turn.

4 Get six correct answers to win!

2 **Now complete your Progress Tracker in the Workbook.**

Workbook page 16

I can use the language in Unit 1. ☐

2 Family and Friends

Lesson 1 Vocabulary

1 **Talk about the picture.**

What shape is this?

It's a heart.

2 1.27 **Listen, point, and say. Then quiz a friend.**

3 1.28 **Listen and point. Then chant.**

My mom and dad,
My brother and sister,
My grandma and
grandpa, too.
All my family,
All my friends,
I love you!

 I can name family members. ☐

Workbook page 17

Lesson 2 Grammar

1 (1.29) **Listen to Nancy and Alex. Then read and say.**

Grammar

Who's this?

This is my grandma.

Who**'s** = Who **is** … ?

Grammar Practice page 106

2 (1.30) **Listen to Nancy and point.**

3 **Sharebook** A: page 13 B: page 13

Family Pictures

 I can ask and answer about family members. ☐

Lesson 3 Story Happy Birthday, Alex!

1 Look and circle.

How old is Alex? He's six. / He's seven.

2 1.31 **Read the story. Then act.**

Value
Be polite!

3 Read and check (✓) the answer.

Thank you!

- You're welcome! ☐
- Nice to meet you! ☐

Lesson 4 Vocabulary

1 (1.32) **Listen, point, and say. Then quiz a friend.**

1 truck

2 bike

3 ball

4 robot

5 car

6 doll

7 kite

2 (1.33) **Listen, point, and sing.**

How Many Toys?

Look at the birthday gifts!
Kites, dolls, and a robot, too.
Balls and a bike! They're great!
Cars and trucks! Thank you!

How many kites? 1, 2, 3!
Three kites! Yes! OK!
What color are they?
They're yellow. Hooray!

3 **Draw and say.**

What is it?

It's a blue robot.

I can name toys. ☐

Workbook page 20

1 Listen, read, and say.
1.34

2 Look at Activity 2 on page 24. Listen and write.
1.35

1 ____________________

2 ____________________

3 ____________________

Grammar

How many cars?	**Three** cars.
What color **are they**?	**They're** red.

one car / two car**s**

They**'re** = They **are**

Grammar Practice page 106

3 Sharebook
A: page 15
B: page 16

How Many Toys?

I can ask and answer about toys. ☐

Lesson 6 Social Studies

CLIL

1 **Look. How many boys and girls in each family?**

2 (1.36) **Read the text. Is your family the same or different?**

Families

1 This is my family.
The **man** is my dad.
The **woman** is my mom.
The **boy** is my brother,
and I'm the **girl**.

2 This is my friend, Maria.
Her family is different.
Two boys and two girls!
Nine **people**!

3 How many people are
in your family?

 I can read about families. ☐

Workbook page 22

Lesson 7 Social Studies

1 (1.37) **Read the text again.**

2 Read and match.

1 three boys
2 one boy
3 two girls
4 one girl

a

b

c

d

3 Project Draw a picture of your family.

4 Share it! Talk about your picture with the class.

This is my grandma.

Share at Home
Spell six family words.

Workbook page 23

I can share my picture. ☐

Lesson 8 Phonics Dd, Ee, Ff

1 Listen, point, and chant.
1.38

2 Listen and repeat. Then read and say.
1.39

1	D	d	E	e	F	f
2	e	F	d	f	D	E

REVIEW

3	A	B	C	B	C	A
4	a	b	c	a	c	b

3 Look and listen. Circle the first letter.
1.40

1 d e f

2 d e f

3 d e f

4 d e f

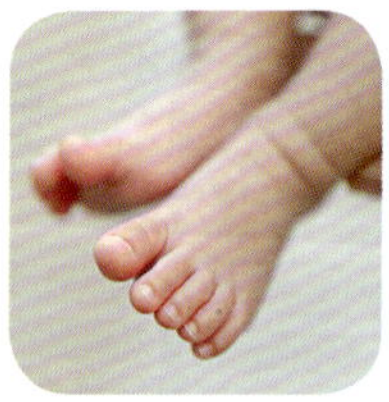

5 d e f

4 Listen, read, and say.
1.41

A fox in a box? Yes, yes, yes.
A duck in a box? Yes.
A dog in a box? Yes, yes, yes.
An elephant in a box? No!

I can read the letters Dd, Ee, and Ff. ☐

Workbook page 24

1 Play *Race to Win!* Use the language from Unit 2.

How to Play

1 Flip a coin. Move one or two spaces.

2 Look, read, and answer.

3 Don't know? Lose a turn.

4 Finish first to win!

move one space

move two spaces

2 **Now complete your Progress Tracker in the Workbook.**

Workbook page 25

I can use the language in Unit 2. ☐

Share the World 1

A Surprise for You!

1 **Look at the pictures. What toys do you see?**

2 **Read the poem. How many dolls are on the table?**

1.42

1 One big doll on the table.
Red, green, and yellow, too.
Open the doll and look inside.
Surprise! Two dolls for you!

2 Two big dolls on the table.
Red, green, and yellow, too.
Open the doll and look inside.
Surprise! Three dolls for you!

3 Three dolls on the table.
Red, green, and yellow, too.
Open the doll and look inside.
Surprise! Four dolls for you!

4 Nine dolls on the table.
Red, green, and yellow, too.
Open the doll and look inside.
A very small doll for you!

3 Read and circle.

1 The poem is about **a book** / **a toy**.

2 There are **nine dolls** / **ten dolls**.

3 The dolls are **all the same** / **all different**.

4 The dolls are **red, green, and yellow** / **red, green, and white**.

4 Share Your World **What's your favorite toy? Draw it in your Workbook.**

Workbook pages 26–27

YLE Starters

Exam Practice 1

Listening

1 (1.43) **Listen and draw lines. There is one example.**

grandma grandpa dad

mom sister brother

Reading and Writing

2 Look and read. Put a tick (✓) or a cross (✗) in the box. There are two examples.

Examples

This is a blue pencil case. ✓

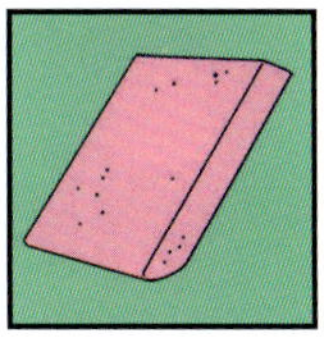

This is a crayon. ✗

Questions

1 

This is a white clock. ☐

2 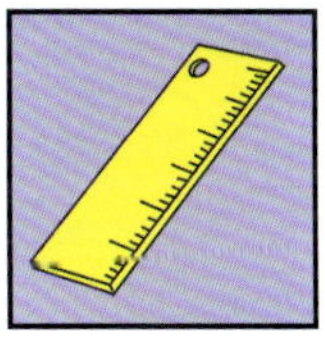

This is an orange ruler. ☐

3 

Three tables. ☐

4 

Two robots. ☐

5 

This is an eraser. ☐

3 Jobs

Lesson 1 Vocabulary

1 Talk about the picture.

How many Share Pals?

Six!

2 1.44 **Listen, point, and say. Then quiz a friend.**

3 1.45 **Listen and point. Then chant.**

A vet! Wow!
A cook! Cool!
A vet, a cook,
And a doctor, too!

A farmer! Wow!
An artist! Cool!
A farmer, an artist,
And a teacher, too!

Lesson 2 Grammar

1 1.46 **Listen to Alex and Nancy. Then read and say.**

Grammar

He**'s** / She**'s** a vet.

He / She **isn't** a vet.

He**'s** = He **is** She**'s** = She **is**

Grammar Practice page 107

2 1.47 **Listen, look, and say *True* or *False*.**

3 **Sharebook** A: page 17 B: page 18

Find Four Differences

Workbook page 29

I can talk about jobs. ☐

Lesson 3 Story I'm Sorry, Eva!

1 Look and circle.

Dan is a vet. Yes, he is. / No, he isn't.

2 1.48 **Read the story. Then act.**

Value
Say sorry!

3 Read and check (✓) the answer.

I'm sorry!

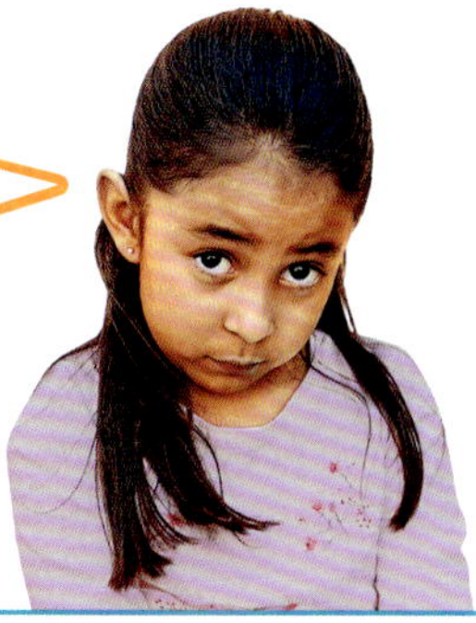

It's OK. ☐

I'm OK. ☐

Workbook page 30

I can read the story. ☐

Lesson 4 Vocabulary

1 1.49 **Listen, point, and say. Then quiz a friend.**

1 firefighter

2 pilot

3 bus driver

4 dentist

5 astronaut

6 singer

7 police officer

8 mail carrier

2 1.50 **Listen and circle. Then mime and sing.**

The Jobs Song

Is he a bus driver?
I don't know!
Is he a  /  ?
No! No! No!
Is he a  /  ?
Yes, he is! He's a dentist.
Now we know!

Is she a  /  ?
I don't know!
Is she a pilot?
No! No! No!
Is she an  /  ?
Yes, she is! She's an astronaut.
Now we know!

3 **Mime a job. Guess!**

She's a singer!

Yes!

Workbook page 31

1 Listen, read, and say.

1.51

Grammar

Is he / she a mail carrier?

Yes, he / she **is**.

No, he / she **isn't**.

Grammar Practice page 107

2 Look at Activity 1 on page 38. Listen and check (✔).

1.52

1		2		3	
Yes	☐	Yes	☐	Yes	☐
No	☐	No	☐	No	☐

3 Sharebook (A: page 19, B: page 21) *Guess the Job*

I can ask and answer about jobs. ☐

Lesson 6 Social Studies

CLIL

1 Look. How many types of transportation do you see?

2 (1.53) **Read the text. What's a tuk-tuk?**

Jobs in the Community

1 This is Decha. He's a **taxi** driver. His taxi is a tuk-tuk. It's a **motorcycle** and a taxi.

2 Gan is a firefighter. His **fire truck** is red and white. It's cool!

3 Mary isn't a pilot. She's a flying doctor. This is her **plane**.

 I can read about jobs in the community. ☐

Workbook page 33

Lesson 7 Social Studies

CLIL

1 (1.54) **Read the text again.**

2 **Read and circle.**

1 Decha is a **bus driver** / **taxi driver**.

2 The fire truck is **yellow** / **red**.

3 Mary is a **pilot** / **doctor**.

3 **Project** **Make a poster of jobs in your community.**

4 **Share it!** **Talk about your poster with the class.**

He's a mail carrier. She's a police officer.

Share at Home
Name six jobs and four types of transportation.

Workbook page 34

I can share my poster. ☐

Lesson 8 Phonics Gg, Hh, Ii

1 Listen, point, and chant.
1.55

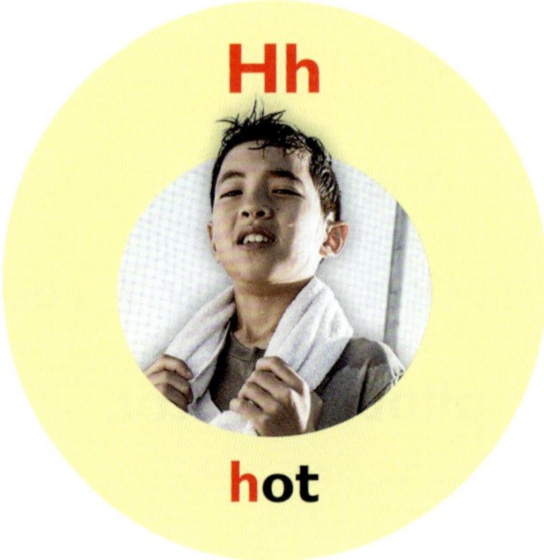

2 Listen and repeat. Then read and say.
1.56

1	G	g	H	h	I	i
2	h	I	g	i	G	H

REVIEW

3	B	C	A	F	D	E
4	a	b	f	e	c	d

3 Look and listen. Circle the first letter.
1.57

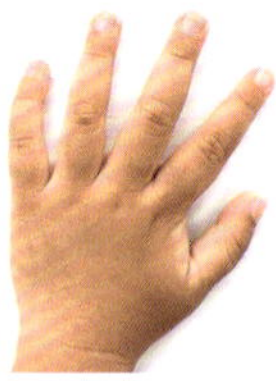

1 g h i   2 g h i   3 g h i   4 g h i   5 g h i

4 Listen, read, and say.
1.58

The goat is green,
The hippo is hot,
The insect is ill,
But the girl is not!

 I can read the letters Gg, Hh, and Ii. ☐ Workbook page 35

1 Play *Four in a Row!* Use the language from Unit 3.

How to Play

1 Collect eight markers.

2 Choose a space. Look, read, and answer.

3 Put a marker on the space.

4 Get four markers in a row to win.

2 **Now complete your Progress Tracker in the Workbook.**

Workbook page 36

I can use the language in Unit 3. ☐

4 At Home

Lesson 1 Vocabulary

1 **Talk about the picture.**

Who's this?

Eva!

2 2.01 **Listen, point, and say. Then quiz a friend.**

3 2.02 **Listen and point. Then chant.**

Friends in the living room,
One. Two. Three.
In the bathroom, in
the bedroom,
They want to play with me!

Friends in the dining room,
In the garage, too.
In the kitchen, in the yard,
They want to play with you!

 I can name the rooms of a house. ☐

Workbook page 37

Lesson 2 Grammar

1 2.03 **Listen to Nancy and May. Then read and say.**

Grammar

Where's your grandpa?

He's **in** the living room.

Where'**s** = Where **is**

Grammar Practice page 107

2 2.04 **Look and listen to May. Say *True* or *False*.**

3 Sharebook A: page 23 B: page 24

Find Your Friends!

 I can ask and answer about where people are. ☐

Lesson 3 Story Hide and Seek!

1 Look and circle.

Sally is in the kitchen. Yes, she is. / No, she isn't.

2 2.05 **Read the story. Then act.**

Value
Show respect!

3 Look, read, and check (✓). Who shows respect?

1 Please be quiet. ☐

2 Oh! Excuse me. ☐

3 Sam is in the garage! ☐

I can read the story. ☐

Lesson 4 Vocabulary

1 2.06 **Listen, point, and say. Then quiz a friend.**

1 TV

2 closet

3 bed

4 sofa

5 bathtub

6 lamp

7 refrigerator

8 rug

2 2.07 **Listen and point. Then mime and sing.**

Where's the Ball?

Where's the ball?
Is it in the  ? No!
Is it in the  ?
No! No! No!

Is it on the  ?
Is it on the  ? No!
Is it on the  ?
Yes! Let's go!

3 **Ask and answer about your house.**

Where's the TV?

It's in the living room.

 I can name things at home. ☐ Workbook page 40

1 2.08 **Listen, read, and say.**

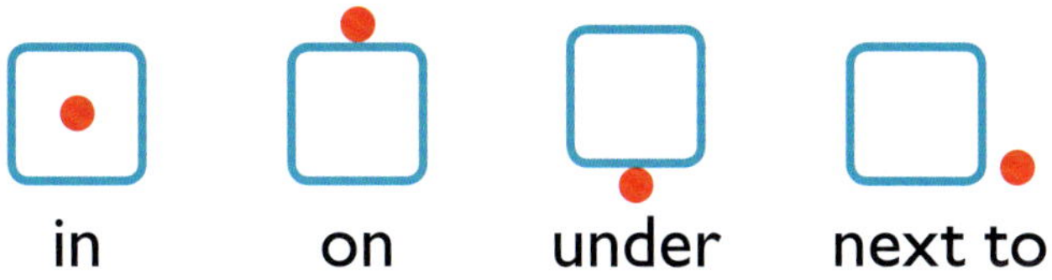

Grammar

Where's your backpack?

It's on the sofa.

Where are your books?

They're next to the lamp.

Grammar Practice page 107

2 **Look for things in your classroom. Ask and answer.**

3 **Sharebook** A: page 25 B: page 26 ***Find the Differences***

 I can ask and answer about where things are. ☐

Lesson 6 Social Studies

CLIL

1 **Look. How many houses do you see?**

2 2.09 **Read the text. Which houses have one room?**

Houses in Nature

1 Look at this house! It has a lot of **flowers**. They're next to the house, in the house, and on the house! This house has six rooms.

2 This house is in a **tree**. There is one room. It's a kitchen, a living room, and a bedroom, too!

3 This house is on the **water**. It has two rooms.

4 This is a greenhouse. It has one room. There are a lot of **plants** in this house!

I can read about houses in nature. ☐

Workbook page 42

Lesson 7 Social Studies

1 Read the text again. 2.10

2 Read and circle *Yes* or *No*.

1 The greenhouse has one room. Yes / No

2 The house on the water has two rooms. Yes / No

3 The house with a lot of flowers has one room. Yes / No

4 The house in the tree has one room. Yes / No

3 **Project** **Draw a picture of a house in nature. How many rooms?**

4 **Share it!** **Talk about your picture with the class.**

This is the kitchen.

Share at Home

Name the rooms in your house and one thing in each room.

Workbook page 43

I can share my picture. ☐

Lesson 8 Phonics Jj, Kk, Ll

1 Listen, point, and chant.
2.11

2 Listen and repeat. Then read and say.
2.12

1	J	j	K	k	L	l
2	k	L	j	l	J	K

REVIEW

3	G	H	I	F	D	E
4	d	e	i	f	g	h

3 Look and listen. Circle the first letter.
2.13

1 j k l

2 j k l

3 j k l

4 j k l

5 j k l

4 Listen, read, and say.
2.14

The kangaroo can jump.
The boy can kick.
The lion can roar,
And the kitten can lick.

I can read the letters Jj, Kk, and Ll. ☐

Workbook page 44

1 Play *Round and Round!* Use the language from Unit 4.

How to Play

1 Spin. Then move your marker.
2 Look, read, and answer.
3 Blue space = 1 point.
4 Yellow space = 2 points.
5 Get 10 points to win!

2 Now complete your Progress Tracker in the Workbook.

Workbook page 45

I can use the language in Unit 4. ☐

Share the World 2

The Red Envelope

1 Look at the pictures. What festival is this? Circle.

Lunar New Year / Mother's Day

2 2.15 **Read the story. What is Yan's present?**

3 **Read and circle *True* or *False*.**

1 New Year is Yan's favorite festival. True / False

2 In picture 3, Yan is in the living room. True / False

3 In picture 5, the present is in the kitchen. True / False

4 In picture 6, the cat is in the yard. True / False

4 **Share Your World** **What's your favorite festival? Draw it in your Workbook.**

Workbook pages 46–47

Listening

1 2.16 **Listen and color. There is one example.**

Reading and Writing

2 Look and read. Write yes or no. There is one example.

Example

The bedroom is next to the living room. ......yes......

Questions

1 The boy is in the bathroom. ....

2 The girl is at the table. ....

3 The artist is on the sofa. ....

4 The father is in the kitchen. ....

5 My Pets

Lesson 1 Vocabulary

1 **Talk about the picture.**

Where's the cat?

It's next to Sam.

2 (2.17) **Listen, point, and say. Then quiz a friend.**

3 (2.18) **Listen and point. Then chant.**

Animals in the pet shop,
A dog, a cat, a fish,
A bird, a mouse, a turtle,
A spider and … what's this?
It's a snake!
SSSSSS!

 I can name pets. ☐

Workbook page 48

Lesson 2 Grammar

1 2.19 **Listen to Nancy and Dan. Then read and say.**

Grammar

I **have** a cat.

I **don't have** a cat.

do**n't** = do **not**

Grammar Practice page 108

2 2.20 **Look, listen, and point.**

3 **Sharebook** A: page 27 B: page 27

Who Am I?

I can talk about pets. ☐

Lesson 3 Story Animals Are Friends

1 Look and circle.

May is nice to animals. Yes, she is. / No, she isn't.

2 2.21 **Read the story. Then act.**

Value
Be nice!

3 Look, read, and check (✓). Who is nice?

1 I'm your friend. ☐

2 Look at the turtle! ☐

3 Here you go. ☐

I can read the story. ☐

Lesson 4 Vocabulary

1 2.22 **Listen, point, and say. Then quiz a friend.**

1 old

2 young

3 long

4 short

5 big

6 small

7 ugly

8 cute

2 2.23 **Listen and point. Then sing.**

The Animal Song

Big and small,
Old and young,
Ugly and cute,
Short and long.

Dogs and cats,
Turtles and mice,
Spiders and fish,
Pets are nice!

3 **Mime an animal. Guess!**

A small bird?

Yes!

Workbook page 51

1 2.24 **Listen, read, and say.**

2 2.25 **Listen and number.**

a  ☐ b  ☐ c  ☐

Grammar

Do you **have** a cat?

Yes, I **do**. / No, I **don't**.

Grammar Practice page 108

3 **Sharebook** A: page 29 B: page 31 ***Go Fish!***

I can ask and answer about pets. ☐

Lesson 6 Art

CLIL

1 **Look. Which shapes do you see?**

2 **Read the text. What shape is the panda's head?**

2.26

Drawing with Shapes

1 This **peacock** is beautiful! You can see triangles, and circles.

2 This **panda** is big! How many circles do you see?

3 This **squirrel** is cute. You can see the squares! Pictures on a computer are small squares.

4 Can you draw an **iguana** with shapes? Which shapes?

 I can read about drawing with shapes. ☐

Workbook page 53

1 2.27 **Read the text again.**

2 **Read and circle.**

1 You can see circles and **squares** / **triangles** in the picture of the squirrel.

2 You can see **squares** / **circles** in the picture of the panda.

3 You can see **circles** / **squares** in the picture of the peacock.

3 **Project Draw an animal picture with shapes.**

4 **Share it! Talk about your picture with the class.**

This is a dog. You can see squares and rectangles.

Share at Home
Talk about your animal picture.

Workbook page 54

I can share my picture. ☐

Lesson 8 Phonics Mm, Nn, Oo

1 Listen, point, and chant.
2.28

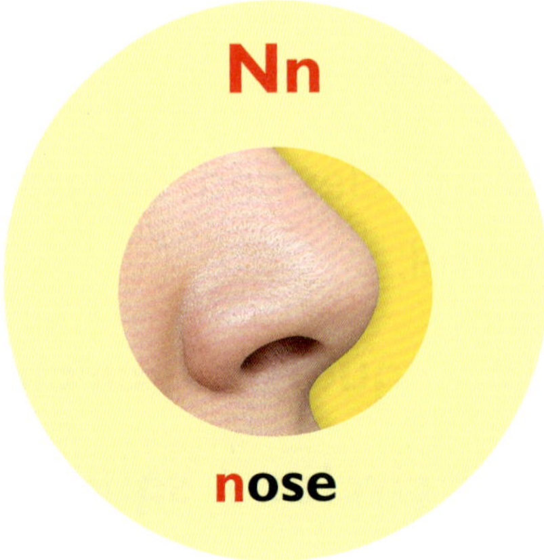

2 Listen and repeat. Then read and say.
2.29

1	M	m	N	n	O	o
2	n	O	m	o	M	N

REVIEW

3	H	G	I	J	L	K
4	i	j	g	h	k	l

3 Look and listen. Circle the first letter.
2.30

1 m n o 2 m n o 3 m n o 4 m n o 5 m n o

4 Listen, read, and say.
2.31

The moon is in the sky.
The nest is in the tree.
The nut is with the mouse.
What else can you see?

 I can read the letters Mm, Nn, and Oo. ☐ Workbook page 55

1 Play *Spin to Win!* Use the language from Unit 5.

How to Play

1 Spin with a pencil and paper clip.

2 Look, read, and answer.

3 Don't know? Lose a turn.

4 Get six correct answers to win!

2 **Now complete your Progress Tracker in the Workbook.**

Workbook page 56

I can use the language in Unit 5. ☐

6 At the Fair

Lesson 1 Vocabulary

1 **Talk about the picture.**

What are these?

They're clowns.

2 2.32 **Listen, point, and say. Then quiz a friend.**

3 2.33 **Listen and point. Then chant.**

Move your fingers!
Move your arms!
Move your hands! Hi!

Move your head!
Move your legs!
Move your feet! Goodbye!

 I can name parts of the body. ☐ Workbook page 57

Lesson 2 Grammar

1 2.34 **Listen to Alex and Nancy. Then read and say.**

Grammar

He **has** big feet.

He **doesn't have** big hands.

doesn**'t** = does **not**

Grammar Practice page 108

2 2.35 **Look at the clowns. Listen and say *True* or *False*.**

3 **Sharebook** A: page 33 B: page 33

Guess the Robot

I can talk about parts of the body. ☐

Lesson 3 Story Look Out, Dan!

1 Look and circle.

Dan helps May. Yes, he does. / No, he doesn't.

2 2.36 **Read the story. Then act.**

Value
Be careful!

3 Look, read, and check (✓). Who is careful?

1 Dan ☐

2 Sally ☐

3 Alex ☐

Lesson 4 Vocabulary

1 2.37 **Listen, point, and say. Then quiz a friend.**

1 eyes

2 ears

3 nose

4 mouth

5 hair

6 teeth

2 2.38 **Listen and point. Then point and sing.**

Point to Your Face!

Point to your head – one!
Point to your eyes – one, two!
Point to your nose – one!
Point to your ears
– one, two!
Point to your mouth.
This is fun!

Point to your hair.
Point to your teeth, too!
Point to your hair, eyes,
nose, ears, mouth, head,
and teeth!
Phew!

3 **Watch your partner. Say the words in order.**

Nose, ears, mouth, eyes!

 I can name parts of the face. ☐ Workbook page 60

1 2.39 **Listen, read, and say.**

2 2.40 **Listen and number.**

a  ☐

b  ☐

c  ☐

Grammar

Does it **have** big eyes?

Yes, it **does**.

No, it **doesn't**.

Grammar Practice page 108

3 **Sharebook** A: page 35 B: page 35 ***Three Questions***

I can ask and answer about faces. ☐

Lesson 6 Science

CLIL

1 **Look. What do you see in the garden?**

2 **Read the text. What are the five senses?**

2.41

The Five Senses

1 I'm in the yard. I can **see** a tree. I see with my eyes.

2 I can **smell** flowers. I smell with my nose.

3 I can **hear** the birds. I hear with my ears.

4 I can **touch** the orange. I touch with my hands and fingers.

5 I can smell the orange. I can **taste** the orange, too. Mmmmm. Yummy!

6 We have five senses. We see, we smell, we hear, we touch, and we taste.

I can read about the five senses. ☐

Workbook page 62

Lesson 7 Science

1 Read the text again. 2.42

2 Match the words with the parts of the body.

1 see
2 hear
3 smell
4 taste
5 touch

a 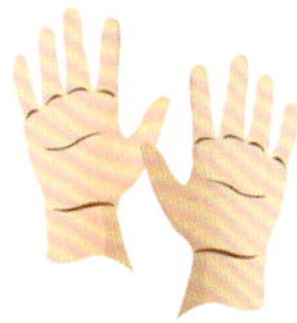

b 

c 

d 

e 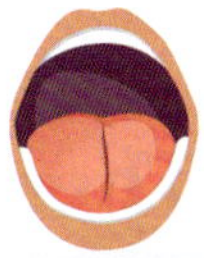

3 Project Draw pictures of your favorite things to see, smell, hear, touch, and taste.

4 Share it! Talk about your picture with the class.

I see my bed.

Share at Home

Say what you see, smell, hear, touch, and taste in your house.

I can share my picture. ☐

Lesson 8 Phonics Pp, Qq, Rr

1 (2.43) Listen, point, and chant.

Pp

pencil

Qq

queen

Rr

red

2 (2.44) Listen and repeat. Then read and say.

1	P	p	Q	q	R	r
2	q	R	p	r	P	Q

REVIEW

3	N	O	M	K	L	J
4	l	m	n	o	j	k

3 (2.45) Look and listen. Circle the first letter.

1 p q r

2 p q r

3 p q r

4 p q r

5 p q r

4 (2.46) Listen, read, and say.

One purple pencil,
Two purple rings, and
Three purple penguins
Are very strange things!

I can read the letters Pp, Qq, and Rr. ☐

Workbook page 64

1 Play ***Race to Win!*** Use the language from Unit 6.

START

m__uth

Spell it.

Does it have ...?

Name it.

It has ...

Does she have ...?

e__es

Spell it.

Lose a turn!

Name it.

It doesn't have ...

Name it.

he__d

Spell it.

It has ...

FINISH

How to Play

1. Flip a coin. Move one or two spaces.
2. Look, read, and answer.
3. Don't know? Lose a turn.
4. Finish first to win!

move one space

move two spaces

2 Now complete your Progress Tracker in the Workbook.

Workbook page 65

I can use the language in Unit 6. ☐

Share the World 3

1 **Look at the pictures. What do koalas eat?**

2 (2.47) **Read the text. Where does the baby koala live?**

Koalas Are Cute!

1 Koalas are from Australia. They live in trees. They have big heads and big noses. They don't have hair. They have fur.

2 They can climb. They eat leaves. They sleep a lot.

3 The mother koala has a pouch. The baby koala lives in the pouch. Baby koalas are very small!

4 Koalas are small and cute, but they have big teeth and big claws. Don't touch a koala!

3 Read and circle *Yes* or *No*.

1 Do koalas live in trees? Yes / No

2 Do they eat oranges? Yes / No

3 Do they have big teeth? Yes / No

4 Are they good pets? Yes / No

4 Share Your World What's your favorite animal? Draw it in your Workbook.

Workbook pages 66–67

YLE Starters

Exam Practice 3

Listening

1 (2.48) **Listen and tick (✔) the box. There is one example.**

Example

What is the pet?

A ☐ B ☐ C ☑

Questions

1 What fish is it?

A ☐ B ☐ C ☐

2 What doll is it?

A ☐ B ☐ C ☐

3 What is in the backpack?

A ☐ B ☐ C ☐

Reading and Writing

2 Look at the pictures. Look at the letters. Write the words. There is one example.

Example

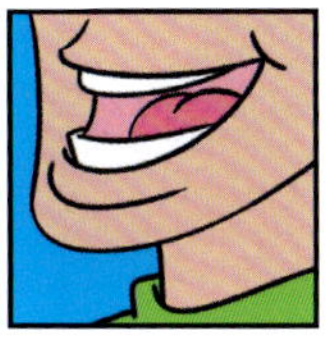

mouth ....

t m h u o

Questions

1 

....

h f s i

2 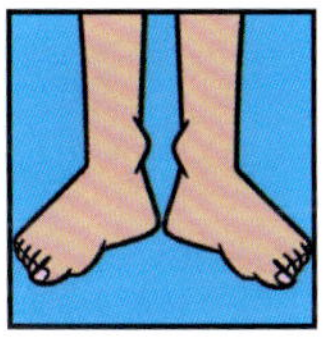

....

e t e f

3 

....

h r a i

4 

....

r d s i p e

5 

....

k e n a s

7 At the Park

Lesson 1 Vocabulary

1 Talk about the picture.

How many dogs?

Two dogs!

2 3.01 **Listen, point, and say. Then quiz a friend.**

3 3.02 **Listen and point. Then chant.**

Men, women, and children,
We're in the park today.
Come to the park. It's fun!
Come to the park and play!

Swings, slides, and a seesaw,
We're in the park today.
Picnic tables and a lake,
Come to the park and play!

 I can name things at the park. ☐

Workbook page 68

Lesson 2 Grammar

1 (3.03) **Listen to Eva and Alex. Then read and say.**

Grammar

There's a slide.

There are swings.

There**'s** = There **is**

Grammar Practice page 109

2 (3.04) **Listen, look, and say *True* or *False*.**

3 Sharebook A: page 37 B: page 38

Find Five Differences

I can talk about the park. ☐

Lesson 3 Story Wash Your Hands!

1 Look and circle.

Dan has mud on his hands. Yes, he does. / No, he doesn't.

2 3.05 **Read the story. Then act.**

Value
Help others!

3 Read and check (✔) the answer.

Let me help you.

I'm clean. ☐

OK, thanks. ☐

Lesson 4 Vocabulary

1 3.06 **Listen, point, and say. Then quiz a friend.**

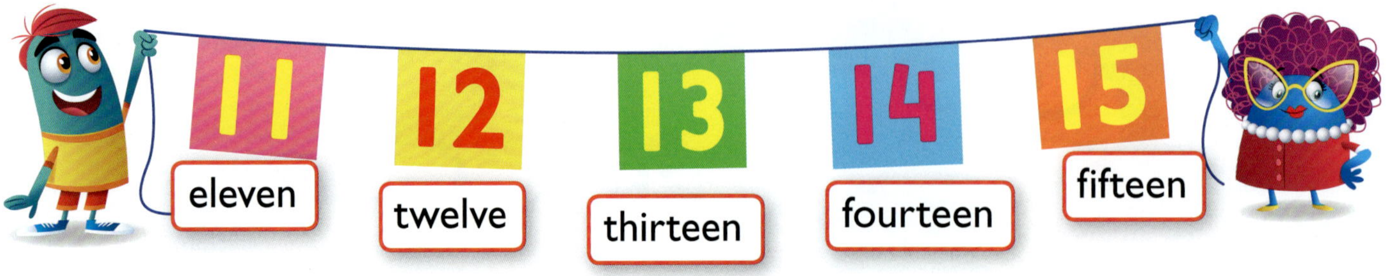

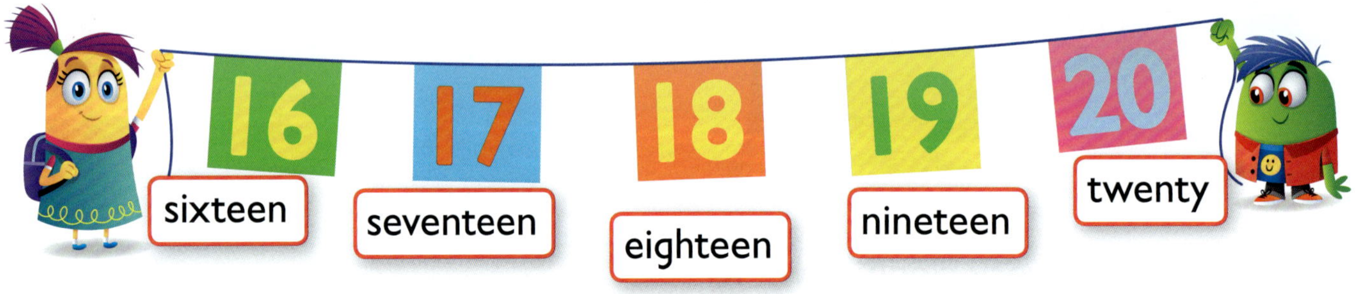

2 3.07 **Listen and count the birds. Then sing.**

Birds in the Park

Let's count the birds.
Let's sing, too!
How many birds are there
in the park with you?

1, 2, 3, 4, 5, 6, 7, 8, 9, 10,
11, 12, 13, 14, 15, 16, 17, 18, 19, 20!
Twenty birds in the park.
Twenty birds with you!

3 **Listen and say the next three numbers.**

Fourteen.

Fifteen, sixteen, seventeen!

 I can count to twenty. ☐ Workbook page 71

1 Listen, read, and say.

3.08

Grammar

How many children **are there**?

There are seven.

How many cake**s** **are there**?

There's one.

Grammar Practice page 109

2 Ask and answer about things in your classroom.

How many chairs are there?

There are 18.

3 Sharebook

A: page 39
B: page 40

Animal Lake

I can ask and answer about things in the park. ☐

Lesson 6 Math CLIL

1 Look. Can you say the answers?

2 Read the text. What are the symbols for *plus* and *minus*? 3.09

Math in English!

1 Can you count from one to twenty? From twenty to one?

2 Now let's do math in English!
There are five girls in the yard.
There are eight boys in the yard, too.
How many children are there in the yard?
This is the **equation**.

5	+	8	=	13
five	**plus**	eight	**equals**	thirteen

3 Let's do another equation.
There are twenty cakes on the table.
You eat three cakes.
How many cakes are there on the table now?

20	–	3	=	17
twenty	**minus**	three	**equals**	seventeen

 I can read about math in English. ☐

Workbook page 73

1 (3.10) **Read the text again.**

2 **Write the missing letters. Then say.**

1 16 + 2 = 18 — S__xteen plus two equals e__ghteen.

2 12 + 5 = 17 — Twelve pl__s five equ__ls seventeen.

3 18 – 3 = 15 — Eighteen minus th__ee equals fi__teen.

4 16 – 4 = 12 — Sixteen m__nus four equals tw__lve.

3 **Project** **Make a math quiz.**

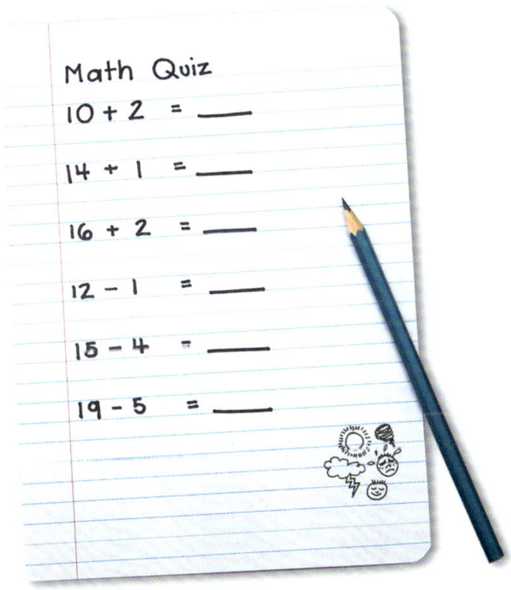

4 **Share it!** **Share your quiz with the class.**

Number one. Ten plus two equals … ?

Share at Home
Ask your family math questions.

Workbook page 74

I can share my math quiz. ☐

Lesson 8 Phonics Ss, Tt, Uu, Vv

1 3.11 **Listen, point, and chant.**

Ss

sit

Tt

train

Uu

umbrella

Vv

van

2 3.12 **Listen and repeat. Then read and say.**

1	S	s	T	t	U	u	V	v
2	t	U	s	v	S	V	T	u

REVIEW

3	R	P	Q	M	O	N
4	o	r	q	n	m	p

3 3.13 **Look and listen. Circle the first letter.**

1 s t u v

2 s t u v

3 s t u v

4 s t u v

5 s t u v

4 3.14 **Listen, read, and say.**

The sun goes up,
The spider goes down,
And the train goes fast
All around the town.

 I can read the letters Ss, Tt, Uu, and Vv. ☐ Workbook page 75

1 Play *Four in a Row!* Use the language from Unit 7.

How to Play

1 Collect eight markers.
2 Choose a space. Look, read, and answer.
3 Put a marker on the space.
4 Get four markers in a row to win.

2 **Now complete your Progress Tracker in the Workbook.**

Workbook page 76

I can use the language in Unit 7. ☐

8 A Picnic

Lesson 1 Vocabulary

1 **Talk about the picture.**

Who's this?

It's Grandpa!

2 3.15 **Listen, point, and say. Then quiz a friend.**

3 3.16 **Listen and point. Then chant.**

Let's have a picnic!
What can we eat?
Bread and cake
And salad and meat.

Let's have pizza!
With a lot of cheese,
Candy and ice cream,
Please! Please! Please!

 I can name food. ☐

Workbook page 77

Lesson 2 Grammar

1 3.17 **Listen to May and Alex. Then read and say.**

Grammar

I **like** cheese.

I **don't like** cheese.

Grammar Practice page 109

2 3.18 **Listen to Alex. Point and say *Yuck* or *Mmm*.**

3 Sharebook A: page 41 B: page 43

I Like It!

Workbook page 78

I can talk about food. ☐

Lesson 3 Story Are You OK?

1 Look and circle.

May has a lot of food. Yes, she does. / No, she doesn't.

2 3.19 **Read the story. Then act.**

Value
Eat healthy!

3 Look, read, and check (✓). Which food is healthy?

1 candy ☐ 

2 salad ☐ 

3 ice cream ☐ 

4 cake ☐ 

Workbook page 79

I can read the story. ☐

Lesson 4 Vocabulary

1 3.20 **Listen, point, and say. Then quiz a friend.**

1 milk

2 yogurt

3 water

4 juice

5 rice

6 fish

7 fruit

2 3.21 **Listen and point. Then mime and sing.**

They're Good for You!

I like 
And I like , too!
You can have a lot.
They're very good for you!

I like 
And I like  and , too!
You can have a lot.
They're very good for you!

I like 
And I like , too!
You can have a lot.
They're very good for you! Yum!

3 **Mime a food. Say a clue. Guess!**

It's white.

Yogurt?

Workbook page 80

1 3.22 **Listen, read, and say.**

2 **Look at the pictures on page 96. Ask and answer.**

Grammar

Do you **like** cake?

Yes, I **do**. / No, I **don't**.

Grammar Practice page 109

3 **Sharebook** A: page 45 B: page 45 ***The Food Quiz***

I can ask and answer about food. ☐

Lesson 6 Health CLIL

1 Look. What food do you see?

2 (3.23) Read the text. How many color words can you find?

Eat a Rainbow!

1 A **healthy meal** has a lot of colors. This meal has red, blue, green, and yellow food. It's healthy!

2 This meal isn't healthy. There aren't a lot of colors.

3 This meal has yellow, orange, and green food. It's healthy!

4 Eat a **rainbow**! Eat a lot of colors every day!

5 Be careful! This candy has a lot of colors, but is it healthy?

I can read about healthy food. ☐

Workbook page 82

CLIL Lesson 7 Health

1 3.24 **Read the text again.**

2 Read and circle.

1 The meal in picture 2 **is** / **isn't** healthy.

2 The meal in picture 2 **has** / **doesn't have** a lot of colors.

3 A meal with a lot of colors **is** / **isn't** healthy.

3 Project Make a food rainbow poster.

4 Share it! Talk about your poster with the class.

This is an apple. It's red. It's healthy.

Share at Home

Talk about food you like and don't like. Ask your family questions, too.

I can share my poster. ☐

Lesson 8 Phonics Ww, Xx, Yy, Zz

1 Listen, point, and chant.
3.25

Ww

water

Xx

box

Yy

yellow

Zz

zebra

2 Listen and repeat. Then read and say.
3.26

1	W	w	X	x	Y	y	Z	z
2	x	Y	w	z	W	Z	X	y

REVIEW

3	T	U	S	V	P	R
4	v	r	s	t	p	u

3 Look and listen. Circle the correct letter for each word.
3.27

1 w x y z

2 w x y z

3 w x y z

4 w x y z

5 w x y z

4 Listen, read, and say.
3.28

Zip the zipper up.
Wipe the window down.
Spin the yo-yo all around.
Shh! Don't make a sound.

 I can read the letters Ww, Xx, Yy, and Zz. ☐

Workbook page 84

1 **Play *Round and Round!* Use the language from Unit 8.**

START

I don't like ...

I like ...

Name it.

b__ea__

Spell it.

Do you like ...?

y__gur__

Spell it.

Do you like ...?

Do you like ...?

Lose a turn!

Name it.

How to Play

1 Spin. Then move your marker.
2 Look, read, and answer.
3 Blue space = 1 point.
4 Yellow space = 2 points.
5 Get 10 points to win!

2 **Now complete your Progress Tracker in the Workbook.**

I can use the language in Unit 8. ☐

Picnic in the Jungle

1 Look and say. Which character are you?

Puma

Spider

Snake

Monkey

Turtle

Frogs

Sloths

Birds

2 Read the play. What's the problem?

3.29

All: Welcome to the jungle!
Puma: I'm Puma, and these are my friends!
Frogs: We're Frogs, and that's Spider.
Sloths: We're Sloths, and that's Turtle.
Birds: We're Birds, and that's Snake.
Turtle: Who's this?
Sloths: Is he a fish?
Puma: No, he isn't.
Spider: Is he a monkey?
Puma: Yes, he is. Hello, Monkey. Welcome to my picnic!
Monkey: Thank you. But I don't have food.
Puma: It's OK. We can share! I have meat.
Snake: The spider has salad. He likes salad.
Monkey: I like fruit.
Spider: Me, too! I like fruit.
All: We like fruit, too!
Puma: Oh, no! We don't have fruit.
All: Oh, no!

Snake: Look, there are mangoes in the tree.
Puma: How many mangoes are there?
All: One, two, three … nineteen, twenty!
Turtle: There are twenty mangoes in the tree!
Frogs: Puma! Jump!
Puma: No.
Sloths: Birds! Fly!
Birds: No.
Monkey: I can help! I can climb. I have long arms. Look!
Puma: Hooray! There's fruit for the picnic!
All: Thank you, Monkey!
Monkey: You're welcome!
Puma: Share your world and be nice, too. You can help others, and they can help you!

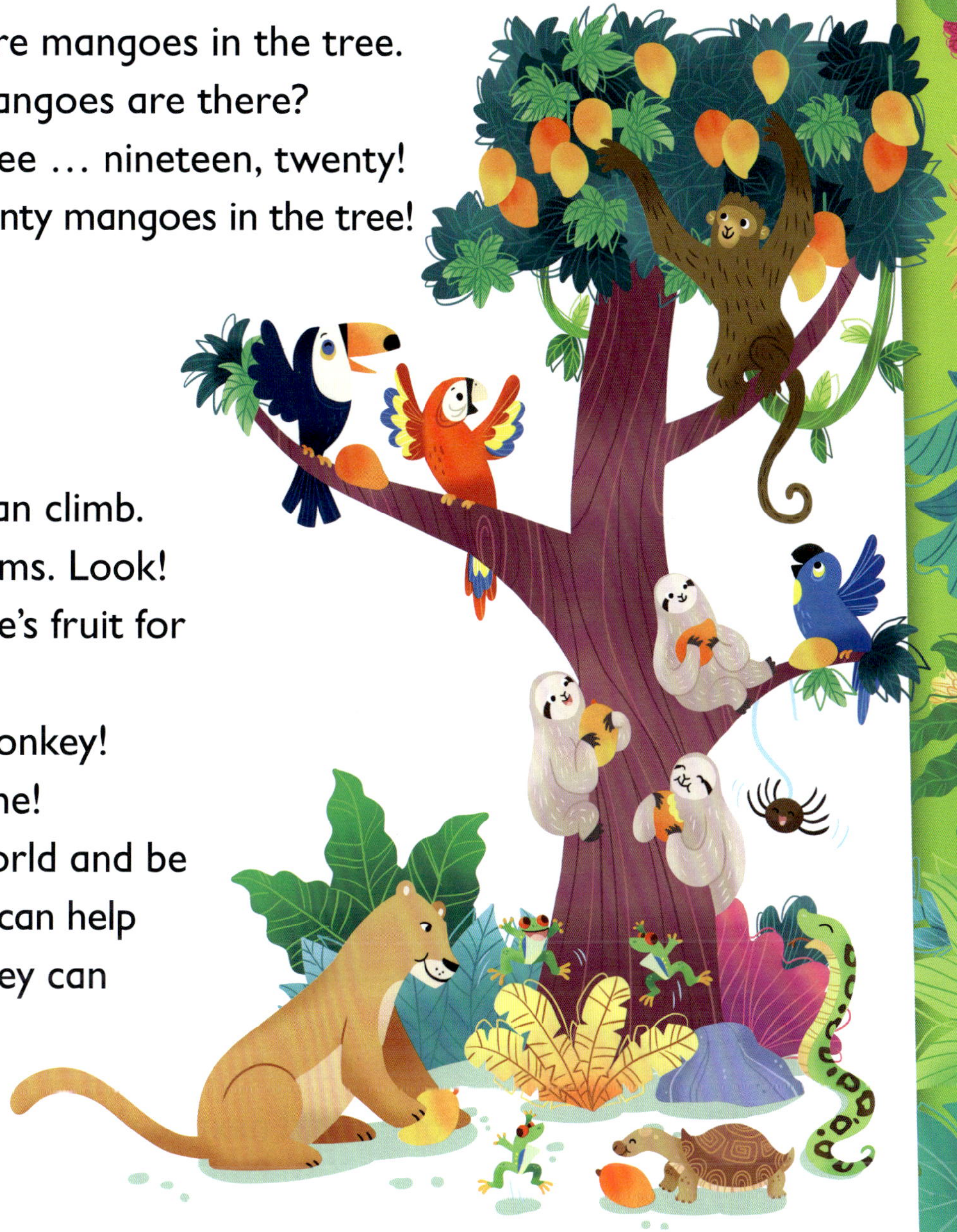

3 Read and circle.

1 The puma **likes** / **doesn't like** meat.

2 The spider has **salad** / **meat**.

3 There are **ten** / **twenty** mangoes in the tree.

4 The animals **have** / **don't have** mangoes at the end.

4 Share Your World **What's your favorite animal in the play? Draw it in your Workbook.**

Workbook pages 86–87

YLE

Starters

Exam Practice 4

Listening

1 3.30 **Read the question. Listen and write a name or number. There are two examples.**

Examples

What is the name of the girl next to the slide? ....Sue........

How old is the girl next to the slide? ....12........

Questions

1 How old is the girl near the lake? ....

2 What is the name of the dog? ....

3 How old is the dog? ....

4 How many cats does the boy have? ....

5 How many swings are there? ....

Reading and Writing

2 Look at the pictures. Look at the letters. Write the words. There is one example.

Example

bread

a r b d e

Questions

1 

....

l e f w r o

2 

....

i c d l h

3 

....

v e t e w l

4 

....

a n d c y

5 

....

o n w m a

Grammar Practice

Unit 1 Lesson 2 (page 11)

What's this?	It's	a blue chair. an orange chair.

Complete.

1 What's ________?
________ a desk.

2 What's ________?
________ a red backpack.

3 ________ this?
It's ________ orange notebook.

Lesson 5 (page 15)

Is it a ruler?	Yes, it is. No, it isn't.

Complete.

1 Is it a pencil case?
Yes, it ________.

2 Is it a crayon?
No, it ________.

3 Is it an eraser?
Yes, ________ ________.

4 ________ it a book?
No, ________ ________.

Unit 2 Lesson 2 (page 21)

Who's this?	This is my dad.

Complete.

1 Who's ________?
This ________ my brother.

2 ________ this?
________ is my friend.

3 ________ ________?
This is my mom.

4 ________ ________?
________ ________ ________ grandma.

Lesson 5 (page 25)

How many balls?		One ball. Four balls.	
What color	is it? are they?	It's They're	green.

Complete.

1 How many robots?
Six ________.

2 What color ________ they?
________ red.

3 How many cars?
One ________.

4 What color ________ it?
________ blue.

Unit 3 Lesson 2 (page 35)

He's She's	a doctor.
He She	**isn't** a cook.

Match.

1 He's a
2 He
3 She's an
4 She isn't

a isn't a teacher.
b artist.
c a farmer.
d vet.

Lesson 5 (page 39)

Is	he she	a pilot?	**Yes**, he **is**. **No**, she **isn't**.

Complete.

1 Is he a dentist?
Yes, he ______.
2 Is he a mail carrier?
No, he ______.
3 Is she a police offer?
Yes, ______ ______.
4 Is she an astronaut?
No, ______ ______.
5 ______ he a singer?
______, he is.

Unit 4 Lesson 2 (page 45)

Where's your friend?	He's She's	**in** the kitchen.

Complete.

1 Where's your dad?
______ in the garage.
2 ______ your sister?
She's ______ the kitchen.
3 ______ your brother?
______ ______ the living room.
4 ______ your grandma?
______ ______ the yard.

Lesson 5 (page 49)

Where's your pen?	**It's**	**in** **on** **under** **next to**	the desk.
Where are your pen**s**?	**They're**		

Complete.

1 Where's your ruler?
______ in my backpack.
2 Where ______ your crayons?
______ on the desk.
3 ______ your pen?
______ under the table.
4 ______ ______ your books?
______ next to the lamp.

Unit 5 Lesson 2 (page 59)

I	have don't have	a fish.

Make true sentences.

1 I __________ a dog.

2 I __________ a cat.

3 I have a __________.

4 I don't have a __________.

5 I __________ a __________.

6 I __________ have a __________.

Lesson 5 (page 63)

Do you have a mouse?	Yes, I do. No, I don't.

Complete.

1 __________ you have a spider?
Yes, I __________.

2 Do you __________ a fish?
No, I __________.

3 __________ you __________ a snake?
__________, I don't.

4 __________ you __________ a bird?
__________, I do.

Unit 6 Lesson 2 (page 69)

He She	has doesn't have	big feet.

Complete.

1 He __________ small hands.
He doesn't __________ big hands.

2 She __________ a big dog.
She __________ have a small dog.

3 He __________ long fingers.
He doesn't __________ short fingers.

4 She __________ long hair.
She __________ have short __________.

Lesson 5 (page 73)

Does it have big teeth?	Yes, it does. No, it doesn't.

Complete.

1 __________ the cat have a cute nose?
Yes, it __________.

2 Does the snake __________ two legs?
No, it __________.

3 __________ the mouse __________ big ears?
No, it __________.

4 __________ the dog __________ teeth?
__________, it does.

Unit 7 Lesson 2 (page 83)

There's	a swing.
There are	two picnic tables.

Complete.

1 There ________ three slides.

2 ________ a picnic table.

3 ________ are two swings.

4 ________ a big lake.

5 There ________ children in the park.

6 ________ ________ flowers, too.

Lesson 5 (page 87)

How many books **are there**?

There are ten.
There's one.

Complete.

1 How many fish are ________?
There ________ seven.

2 How ________ children ________ there?
________ are twelve.

3 ________ many birds ________ ________?
________ one.

Unit 8 Lesson 2 (page 93)

I	**like** **don't like**	pizza.

Make true sentences.

1 I ________ yogurt.

2 I ________ fish.

3 I like ________.

4 I don't like ________.

5 I ________ ________.

6 I ________ like ________.

Lesson 5 (page 97)

Do you **like** salad?	Yes, I **do**. No, I **don't**.

Complete.

1 Do you ________ candy?
Yes, I ________.

2 ________ you like cheese?
No, I ________.

3 Do you like ________?
________, I do.

4 Do ________ like ________?
________, I don't.

YLE words ✔ in BOLD

Word List

a

a 10
a lot of 50
all 20
alphabet 9
an 11
and 7
animal 58
ant 18
apple 18
are 8
arm 68
around 16
artist 34
astronaut 38

b

backpack 10
ball 18, 24
bathroom 44
bathtub 48
be 23
beautiful 60
bed 48
bedroom 44
big 10, 62
bike 24
bird 58
birthday 22
black 7
blue 7
board 10
book 14
box 28
boy 18, 26
bread 92
brother 20
brown 7
bus driver 38

c

cake 92
candle 23
candy 92
car 18, 24
careful 70
cat 18, 58
chair 10
cheese 92
children 82
circle (n) 16
clap (v) 9
claw (n) 79
clean (n) 84
clock 10
closet 48
color (n) 7
color (v) 12
community 40
cook (n) 34
cool 10
crayon 14
cute 62

d

dad 20
dance (v) 9
dentist 38
desk 10
dining room 44
do 59
doctor 34
does 73
doesn't 69
dog 28, 58
doll 24
don't 59
down 90
draw 9
duck 28

e

ears 72
eat 78
egg 28
eight 8
eighteen 86
elephant 28
eleven 86
else 66
equal (v) 88
equation 88
eraser 14
everyone 23
excuse me 47
eyes 72

f

family 20
farmer 34
fast 90
favorite 54
feet 68
festival 54
fifteen 86
fingers 68
fire truck 40
firefighter 38
fish (n) 28, 58, 96
five 8
flowers 50
fly (v) 103
for 10
four 8
fourteen 86
fox 28
friend 20
frog 102
fruit 96
fun 13
fur 78

g

garage 44
girl 26
go 48
goat 42
good 14
goodbye 68
grandma 20
grandpa 20
great 24
green 7
guess (v) 36

h

hair 72
hand 68
happy 22
has 69
have 59
head 68
healthy 94
hear 74
heart 16
hello 4
help 84
here 60
hey 70
hi 4
hippo 42
hot 42
how 8

i

ice cream 92
iguana 64
ill 42
I'm 4
in 14
insect 42
inside 30
is 11
isn't 15
it 11
it's 11

j

job 34
juice 96
jump 52
jungle 102

k

kangaroo 52
kick 52
kitchen 44
kite 24
kitten 52
know 38
koala 78

l

lake 82
lamp 48
leaf 52
leg 68
let's 12
lick 52
like 10
lion 52
little 55
live (v) 78
living room 44
long 62
look 10
love (v) 20

m

mail carrier 38
man 26
mango 103
many 24
me 14
meal 98
meat 92
meet 22

men 82
milk 96
minus 88
mom 20
monkey 66
moon 66
motorcycle 40
mouse 58
mouth 72
move (v) 68
much 22
mud 84
my 4

n

name (n) 4
name's 4
nature 50
nest 66
New Year 54
next to 49
nice 22
nine 8
nineteen 86
no 15
nose 66
not 15
notebook 10
now 37
nut 66

o

octopus 66
OK 14
old 8, 62
on 30
one 8
open (v) 30
orange 7
others 85

p

paint (v) 9
panda 64
park (n) 82
peacock 64
pen 14
pencil 14
pencil case 14
pencil sharpener 14
penguin 76
people 26
pet (n) 58
pick up 14
picnic (n) 92
picnic table 82
picture 10
pilot 38
pink 7
pizza 92
plane 40
plants (n) 50
play (v) 36
please 12
plus 88
point (v) 72
police officer 38
polite 23
pouch 79
present (n) 54
puma 102
purple 7
put 14

q

queen 36
quiet 47

r

rainbow 98
rectangle 16
red 7
refrigerator 48
respect (n) 47
rice 96
ring (n) 76
roar (v) 52
robot 24
rug 48
ruler 14

s

salad 92
say (v) 9
see 46
seesaw 82
seven 8
seventeen 86
share 12
sharing 13
shop (n) 58
short 62
show (v) 14
sing 9
singer 38
sister 20
sit 90
six 8
sixteen 86
sky 66
sleep (v) 78
slide (n) 82
sloth 102
small 62
smell (v) 74
snake 58
sofa 48
sorry 36
sound (n) 100
spell (v) 9
spider 58
spin 100
square 16
squirrel 64
strange 76
sun 90
surprise (n) 30
swing (n) 82

t

table 30
taste (v) 74
taxi 40
teacher 34
teeth 72
ten 8
thank you 12
there are 83
there is 83
there's 83
they 25
they're 25
thing 10
thirteen 86
this 11
three 8
time (n) 10
too 7
touch (v) 74
town 90
train (n) 90
tree 50
triangle 16
truck 24
turn 36
turtle 58
TV 48
twelve 86
twenty 86
two 8

u

ugly 62
umbrella 90
under 49
unhealthy 98
up 100

v

van 90
very 22
vet 34

w

wash 84
water 50, 96
well done 14
what 7
what's 4
where 45
where's 45
white 7
who 21
who's 21
window 10
wipe (v) 100
with 44
woman 26
women 82
wow 13

x

y

yard 44
yellow 7
yes 13
yogurt 96
you 8
young 62
your 4
yo-yo 100

z

zebra 100
zip (v) 100
zipper 100

Macmillan Education Limited
4 Crinan Street
London N1 9XW

Companies and representatives throughout the world

Student Book ISBN 978-1-380-00003-3
Student Book Pack ISBN 978-1-380-02272-1

Written by Nicholas Beare
Phonics lessons written by Wiley Blevins

The author has asserted their right to be identified as the author of this work in accordance with the Copyright, Designs and Patents Act 1988.

Share It! is a registered trademark published by Macmillan Education Limited

First published 2020

Designed by Pronk Media, Inc.
Illustrated by David Belmonte (Beehive Illustration) pp. 32, 33, 56, 57, 80, 81, 104, 105; Dave Cockburn pp. 54–55; Camilla Galindo (Beehive Illustration) pp. 102–103; Keri Green (Beehive Illustration) pp. 18, 19, 28, 29, 42, 43, 52, 53, 66, 67, 76, 77, 90, 91, 100, 101; Patricia Lima pp. 30–31; Emi Ordás & Wedoo Studio pp. 4–5, 6, 7, 8, 9, 10–11, 12–13, 15, 17, 19, 20–21, 22–23, 25, 27, 29, 34–35, 36–37, 39, 41, 43, 44–45, 46–47, 49, 51, 53, 58–59, 60–61, 63, 65, 67, 68–69, 70–71, 73, 75, 77, 82–83, 84–85, 86, 87, 89, 91, 92–93, 94–95, 97, 99, 101; Nicholas Rudnitzky (Beehive Illustration) pp. 14, 15, 24, 38, 48, 62, 63, 64, 72, 75, 86, 96.
Cover design by Roberto Martinez, Marcin Rojek, and Wojciech Szulik
Cover illustration by Emi Ordás
Cover photographs by Getty Images/iStock/ian routledge, Getty Images/iStock/pyotr021
Picture research by Sarah Wells

Author's acknowledgements
The author would like to thank everyone at Macmillan Education and RedNova Learning for their help, ideas, and resourcefulness.

The authors and publishers would like to thank the following for permission to reproduce their photographs:
Alamy Stock Photo/Lisa Strachan p. 98(5), Alamy Stock Photo/marla chebby p. 98(4); Alamy Stock Photo/phil gould p. 79(tr); Alamy Stock Photo/OJO Images Ltd, p. 88(t), Alamy Stock Photo/Vivid Photo Visual p. 64(b); **Brand X** p. 18(br); **Getty Images** p. 42(tr), Getty Images/Blend Images/KidStock p. 85, Getty Images/Caiaimage/Robert Daly p. 27(a), Getty Images/Corbis/Lawrence Manning p. 100(bml), Getty Images/Corbis/VCG/Igor Emmerich p. 26(inset family), Getty Images/Creative Studio Heinemann p. 52(tr), Getty Images/Cultura/Marco Simoni p. 16(main), Getty Images/Cultura/Simon Murrell pp. 28(tr), 52(bl), Getty Images/Digital Vision/Ariel Skelley p. 18(tm), Getty Images/E+/4x6 p. 40(man), Getty Images/E+/Antagain p. 18(bml), Getty Images/E+/mladn61 p. 40(right), Getty Images/E+/NickS p. 40(l), Getty Images/E+/rusm p. 28(bm), Getty Images/E+/skegbydave p. 64(r), Getty Images/E+/Zocha_K p. 16(ml), Getty Images/EyeEm/Abhishek Shanker p. 50(mr), Getty Images/EyeEm/Christian Kreutz p. 100(bmr), Getty Images/EyeEm/Ismail Sadiron p. 28(tm), Getty Images/EyeEm/Saksit Kuson p. 40(woman, r), Getty Images/iStock/amriphoto p. 28(bml), Getty Images/iStock/anankkml p. 66(bm), Getty Images/iStock/Blade_kostas p. 90(tr), Getty Images/iStock/Bloodlinewolf p. 16(r), Getty Images/iStock/bradleyblackburn p. 52(bm), Getty Images/iStock/Catalin205 p. 76(bml), Getty Images/iStock/Cipariss p. 100(bl), Getty Images/iStock/gjohnstonphoto p. 42(tm), Getty Images/iStock/GlobalP pp. 28(bmr), 52(br), 66(tl), 100(tr), Getty Images/iStock/jaroon p. 90(tl), Getty Images/iStock/jax10289 p. 74(main), Getty Images/iStock/johnrandallalves p. 90(bml), Getty Images/iStock/kotomiti p. 76(bmr), Getty Images/iStock/LightFieldStudios p. 76(bm), Getty Images/iStock/Ljupco p. 52(tm), Getty Images/iStock/Maridav p. 16(l), Getty Images/iStock/monkeybusinessimages pp. 26(br), 27(d), Getty Images/iStock/Nynke van Holten p. 18(tr), Getty Images/iStock/obewon p. 52(bml), Getty Images/iStock/rclassenlayouts p. 76(bl), Getty Images/iStock/RuslanDashinsky p. 100(tmr), Getty Images/iStock/RusN pp. 66(tm), 74(3), Getty Images/iStock/scanrail p. 90(tml), Getty Images/iStock/Toxitz p. 52(bmr), Getty Images/iStock/venusphoto p. 98(3), Getty Images/iStock/Vladimiroquai p. 18(bm), Getty Images/iStock/xalanx p. 42(bml), Getty Images/iStockphoto/LUHUANFENG p. 90(bmr), Getty Images/iStockphoto/Pakhnyushchyy p. 66(bmr), Getty Images/iStockphoto/Thinkstock Images/AlexVarlakov p. 42(br), Getty Images/iStockphoto/Thinkstock Images/denphumi p. 66(bl), Getty Images/iStockphoto/Thinkstock Images/Eric IssellÌ©e p. 42(bl), Getty Images/iStockphoto/Thinkstock Images/Mile Atanasov p. 76(br), Getty Images/iStockToprakBeyBetmen p. 90(tmr), Getty Images/JGI/Jamie Grill p. 42(tl), Getty Images/Maisie Paterson/Tetra Images p. 74(2), Getty Images/MITO images/Norbert Achtelik p. 64(r,inset), Getty Images/Moment/Michael Siward p. 78(tr), Getty Images/Moment/Photo by Tse Hon Ning p. 78(br), Getty Images/Moment/R. Tsubin p. 66(br), Getty Images/Moment/Tomekbudujedomek p. 100(br), Getty Images/Moment/Yasser Chalid p. 42(bmr), Getty Images/OJO Images/Sam Edwards p. 27(b), Getty Images/OJO Images/Tom Merton p. 52(tl), Getty Images/Per Magnus Persson p. 50(main), Getty Images/Photodisc/Siede Preis p. 42(bm), Getty Images/Photographer's Choice RF/Tier Und Naturfotografie J und C Sohns p. 64(l), Getty Images/Stockbyte p. 76(tl), Getty Images/Stockbyte/Charles Nesbit p. 76(tr), Getty Images/Tim Graham Photo Library p. 76(tm), Getty Images/TongRo Image Stock RF/Thinkstock Images/TongRo Image Stock p. 100(tl), Getty Images/TongRo Images Inc p. 88(main), Getty Images/Upper Cut Images/Tim Dolan Photography p. 26(bl), Getty Images/Westend61 pp. 26(main), 74(5), 90(bl); **iStockphoto**/nata_vkusidey p. 98(1); **Medio Images**/1996-98 AccuSoft Inc p. 16(t); **Photodisc** p. 28(tl), PhotoDisc/ Getty Images pp. 40(main), 100(bm); **Shutterstock**/alfaori p. 50(br), Shutterstock/Asia Images Group p. 27(c), Shutterstock/Ben Schonewille p. 50(ml), Shutterstock/Bojsha p. 98(main), Shutterstock/Eddie Phantana p. 28(br), Shutterstock/GOLFX p. 74(1), Shutterstock/KDdesignphoto p. 23, Shutterstock/MNStudio p. 74(4), Shutterstock/plavevski p. 79(cl), Shutterstock/PrimePhoto p. 64(tr), Shutterstock/smilepoker p. 40(man, l), Shutterstock/sundatoon p. 79(cr), Shutterstock/takayko photo p. 88(b); **Macmillan Education Limited**/Paul Bricknell p. 18(bl); **Stockbyte** p. 100(tml).

Commissioned photographs by Kikor (pp. 11, 15, 21, 25, 35, 39, 45, 49, 59, 63, 69, 73, 83, 87, 93, 97).

The authors and publishers wish to thank the following for their help with the photo shoot: World of Kids, Inc.; Athena; Ben; Bianca; Jayden; Logan; and Maggie.

Commissioned prop photographs by Luise Johnson-Dailey, Bluwave Creative (pp. 17, 27, 41, 51, 65, 75, 89, 99).

Printed and bound in Brazil.
2025
75